ALEXANDRA POPA

Tiny thoughts

AF286322

Micro Poetry Collection

Tiny Thoughts
Micro Poetry Collection

First printing 2023

IG Pages:
@_the.ephemeral.soul_
@fairy.world.poetry

Herstellung und Verlag:
BoD – Books on Demand, Norderstedt
ISBN: 9783757890148

Dedicated to my beloved husband and
to my two wonderful children

Poetry

Ghosts of poetry

Enthralling endeavor, everlasting ecstasy,
Lettering luminous, my love, my legacy,
Creeping crepuscular in crevasses with calligraphy,
Eerie or elegant, my eloquent epic elegy,
Seamless semantics, sensual, the symmetry,
Rhymes and rhythm, romantic rhapsody,
Behold my beloved, my ghosts of poetry.

I am the page

I am the page, the ink, the poem,
My mind is a poetical reverie and I am lost in it,
I hide my sharp edges and turn them into art,
Everytime I touch my quill and paper
The verses fly smoothly out of my mind,
Like a sweet rebellion of ephemeral fireflies,
They find their peaceful dreams,
On the soft paper printed in aurora hues.

I am made of...

I am made of
Ardent latin blood
Apricot pale skin,
Hazel halcyon eyes,
Golden-fire romantic soul,
Amaranthine coated heart,
Lapislazuli passionate mind,
Viking fighting spirit,
I hold a pen and a blade in my hand
And I am not afraid to use them.

My ink

My ink is made of blue fireflies tears,
Of pastel dewdrops and ruby red roses,
Spilling lines and verses, releasing fears,
On apricot velvet canvas, my soul encloses.

Wounded soul

Wounded sad soul of a poetic kind,
Broken letters, spilled ink in my mind,
Rushing adrenaline, I'm saying it's fine,
Then hitting hard with a bloody rhyme.

Poetical Labyrinth

The labyrinth of my poetic heart,
Is filled with cerulean dreams,
With raven moments, with nocturnal gleams,
The solemn echoes of my fearless wings,
Will turn my sorrows into art.

Inky blood

When my inky blood begins to riot,
My mighty quill begins to dance,
My mind becomes more quiet,
As the letters imprint a romance.

Blooming thoughts

My blooming thoughts are wild and free,
Rose sparkling ink, new writing spree,
Deep roots of art, a verdant canopy,
Releasing me, singing my symphony.

Verses with rhymes are forged so bright,
Scribbling fairytales and trails of light,
They keep me safe, they keep me tight,
With wings of love, my escape flight.

3 a.m. thoughts

3 am thoughts are feeding on me,
Leaving me like a lonely leafless tree,
A glowing wisteria still lurking inside,
Igniting poetical powers, helping me thrive.

Sad Lullaby

My pen sings a lullaby with sadness,
The crimson ink will wipe away my tears,
The verses, fire and water, flowing endless,
In silent seashells, encasing my wild fears.

Lost

Lost between the galaxies of your eyes
I found my name written in invisible ink,
You've painted my heart with their hazel dyes
We felt the love and the cosmic sync.

Vicious blood

The blood running in my veins is so vicious,
My quill starts writing itself, so delicious,
With whiskey scented letters, so malicious,
Angelic rhymes and rhythms, so suspicious.

Pink love potions

Pink love potions and spilled gold ink,
Fusing in my heart's secret chamber,
A lonely poet that just wanted to sync,
But fell in love with her letters of amber.

Mauve melancholy

Wild waves of mauve melancholy,
Are caressing my summer tanned face
You're lonely now in someone's embrace,
And I'm getting high on writing poetry.

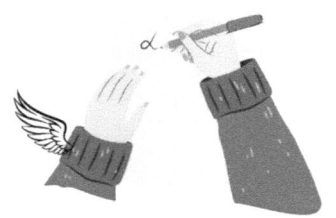

Between my layers

Between my luscious layers of limestone and silk,
My heart is carved out of marble and covered in ink,
Syllables of honey and lemon have painted her walls,
Poetry whispers, echoing in her dim lit halls.

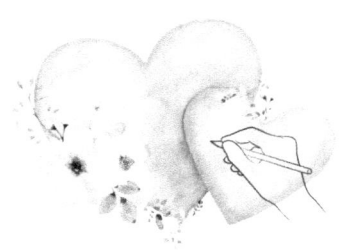

My salvation

The ink spring of my ephemeral soul,
Lies in the depths of my imagination,
When poetry became my salvation,
I finally felt myself like whole.

Purple poems

There are moonbeams in my mind,
Printing purple poems,
I am in a Tri-dimensional awakening
Where blackholes are unraveling breathtaking odysseys,
Attracting everything in their maze.
Although your tumultuous nebula,
Is keeping me prisoner,
I am still the queen of celestial sunsets,
And you are unworthy of my gaze.

Bleeding ink

I'm bleeding ink in shades of autumn amber,
The liquid letters are sparkling like gold,
Igniting passion in my heart's russet chamber,
With bursting rays, my rhymes will unfold.

Mistress of ink

Fatal fragrance of my showered skin,
Silky seduction, you're whirling within,
Dripping desires, into my passion you'll sink,
Alluring aromas, I'm your mistress of ink.

Crimson drops

Crimson dyed drops in snow will spill,
The essence of my trusted frozen quill,
In canopy of blue light, on a rustic hill,
His last murmuration, my poetic kill.

Quiet Letters

Like emerald butterflies
On iridescent tulips,
Are the quiet letters,
Jumping out of my quill,
Entwining the blank pages,
Giving me soft solace
With sparks of afterglow,
My heart they will heal.

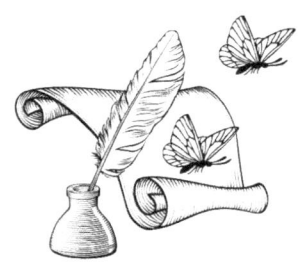

I am a maze

I am a maze, with mirrors
And undiscovered voids,
Confusing and complicated,
My angels and demons
Are dancing on thin ice,
Hidding the reflections of you,
And these flaming feelings,
Between my heart's cassis walls.

Psychedelic pen

Obsessive bliss, inviting temptation,
He beguilingly keeps calling my name,
Can't get no sleep, sinister apparition,
My psychedelic pen is hard to tame.

"Her soul blooms" I hear him say,
Whispering in the darkest hour,
"Here is my wisdom, if you may,
I could be your friend, your armour"

Matrix maze

Matrix maze of memories murmurations,
Melting in my mind, morbid manifestations,
Million minutes and moons of malice,
Mesmerizing musings, mending my madness.

Winds of May

The winds of May remind me you were mine,
Floating free like feathers in a tidal wave,
Titanium souls, scents of juniper, so divine,
The poems in your eyes made me your slave.

Butterfly effect

You have the butterfly effect on me,
Hidden rainbow ribbons tied through poetry,
Your soothing words are heartfelt, reverberating ray,
Waves of sheer sparkles you always send my way.

Poetic tornado

You are the only one,
Who can tame the poetic tornado in me,
When I am whirling the amber leaves,
Tormenting the sand on the dusty roads,
And rising the tender dandelion seeds.

Amaranthine

You wrote your name,
With invisible ink and stardust,
On the canvas of my amaranthine heart.

Blueberry veins

Bleeding ink from my blueberry veins,
Rhymes flowing freely, covering pains,
Flooding my canvas, my poetical garden,
Blooming pastel verses to release my burden.

Butterfly rose

The butterfly rose, stretching its cassis wings,
Flushing through my bridal blossom pages,
Leaving behind a trace of whispering blushing letters,
And diaphanous vanilla scented rhymes,
Caressing my rosaline adorned heart,
With its elixir of life.

Winds of words

I am made of aureate soil,
My pen with passion will boil,
I hide whispers beneath the moon,
Winds of words, synchronising tune.

Poetry for the soul

Poetry surrounding my aching soul,
Had saved me so many times,
When I was lost in neverland,
Or crying in wonderland.
Words, verses, lines and stanzas,
Elevating from me, in glimpses,
Flying high, reaching the moonlight,
Like an opulent embroidery,
Words are stitches for my shattered ventricles.

Wings of poetry

Flying high on the wings of poetry,
My spirit is lifted,
I radiate serenity,
I can see my life from above,
The goods and the bads,
My sugary sides and my dark desires.
From up here,
I understand myself better,
I am my own hero,
Holding swirling rainbows in my hands,
From here the view of my life is ravishing,
I can forgive me for my past mistakes,
The curves and the scars,
Are mine to behold and to cherish.
And when my spirit reunites
With my body,
I will feel revived, untethered soul
And eager to go on, turning a new leaf.

Paint with grey

I no longer paint with grey,
Fifty shades have turned to dust.
My canvas was kissed by autumn's rust,
And dreams of love under an amber ray.

Poet without a pen

I visited your heart today,
To pacify my bittersweet soul,
Passion had again ignited us,
Twin sun-yellow flames,
Unfading passion, timeless love.
I felt sparkles jumping of my fingertips,
Bewitching golden desire,
I wanted to write a poem,
About our elysian limerence,
And then I realised,
In the middle of everything,
That I'm a poet without a pen,
Because I forgot it,
On your flaming cosy bed.

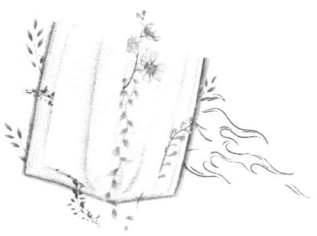

10.000 pages

10.000 pages I imprinted with thoughts,
I finally found a blank one, dusted with quartz,
Then I looked around me, the clouds were seven,
Standing before a gate, on the stairway to heaven.

I am a woman

I am a woman,
Soft soul with a warrior heart,
I might cry or fall apart,
I rise and shine,
Feeling like the world is mine.
I hold my family together,
No matter how's the weather,
I have them sheltered,
And give them kisses, tender.
I fight with dragons and nightmares,
And fever, colds and headaches,
And I never forget about me,
I hold myself when I feel lonely,
Or write some musical poetry.

Flowers

Soft caresses

Your soft caresses remind me
Of buttercream summer clouds
Of jasmine scented perfume,
And hues of gold and tangerine.

Love letters

Love letters in blood and a velvet black rose,
Like a bookstore madness, my delirious prose,
Naked thoughts expressed, I feel so exposed,
The memories of us, just dusted lost echoes.

Goddess

Standing in Aphrodite's temple of labyrinths,
Covering myself with black roses and hyacinths,
Sipping iridescent nights from pretty amphoras,
I've been hiding myself in the chest of Pandora's.

Frozen Queen

I've hidden the tulips, they're poisoned with spring,
The frosted fractals, my heart's symphony will sing,
I'm charmed by the snowflakes, they caress my skin,
With porcelain hands, I'm the frozen Queen,
The bitter arctic winds blow tenderly for me,
Silent hues of auroras will set my spirit free.

White Lilies

White lilies melting on my flawless skin,
I feel their warm core sliding within,
Their ambrosial scent caressing my nose,
Luring me out of my hidden world.

Ebony rose

Alone with myself like an ebony rose,
Reborn from ashes, spring-scented prose,
My verses unfolding with untamed desire,
Molding my sharp edges with reviving fire.

Vanilla skin

Kiss my vanilla skin, under the honeyed moon,
Touch my blushed petals, make me bloom,
I feel sparks of passion on your fingertips,
As you taste my softness with your lustful lips.

Forbidden flowers

Your lips taste like forbidden flowers,
Dewdrops of dawn with magical powers,
Jasmine scented with honeysuckle hues,
Singing to me their enchanting blues.

Purple petunia petals

Horizons bleed in black their evergreen essence,
Pouring purple petunia petals like spears,
The winds whisper with shivering silence,
As weeping willows weep with thorny tears.

And I...

I am murmuring a lonely night rhapsody,
Like a violet wisteria blowing in the wind,
Insatiable tones, a perfect petunia melody,
Longing for your lustful limerence imprint.

October

Stain me like a fire opal dahlia,
Take me with you into your hazel shadows,
Hide me between hues of amber gold,
Caught in your auburn web of sepia leaves,
Dear October, I'll be your subtle possession.

Heaven

Your delicate skin smells like fruity clementine,
And blossoms dipped in candy floss, purely divine,
Chimes of shining bluebells, I hear them in your voice,
You are my earthly heaven, your arms are my rejoice.

Snowdrops soliloquies

I am dreaming dragonflies,
Stained in rainbow hues,
In the gardens of gratitude,
Hoping for the best times.
Thinking about how the seasons
will change my being,
I am listening to the snowdrop soliloquies,
Radiating resilience,
Placing butterfly wishes,
And counting the candy cotton clouds,
I feel unburdened, unblemished, alive.

Spring core

Picking up the moiré pieces of our winter,
I'll dip them in amaranthine and gold,
Lace them with orange blossom splinter,
Plethora of dreams in spring's splendid core.

Sunflowers and daisies

Sahara gold, the color of my ephemeral soul,
Sunflowers and daisies running through my veins,
I will always find my solace in the afterglow,
The iridescent sunbeams are melting my pains.

Pearly tulips

Pearly tender tulips singing to my heart,
They kiss it with softness, make it restart,
Fuel of cotton candy and dulcet lollipops,
Covering my scars with their healing drops.

Magnolia breeze

Mystique of the midnight, the magnolia breeze,
Beauteous silky softness, love's allure tease,
Your fragrant lullaby under the sheer moonlight,
I'm drunk with passion and your hypnotic sight.

Blissful dreams

Blissful dreams and summer time blues,
Lilacs and love letters with alluring hues,
The sea is calling me, enchanting muse,
Staring at the sky, my poetical infuse.

Daisy heart

Just cradle my daisy heart,
Don't promise me forever,
Embrace me in your arms,
Treat me soft and tender.

June waters

Sage green June waters embalming my soul,
In lavender fields I'll be searching my solace,
I know that my flaws will make me shine more,
I'll meet me in forever, I'll get to the surface.

Rainbow raindrops

Rainbow raindrops, exhaling their innocence,
On soft petals of tangerine tulips,
Sweeten the hearts tarnished and tormented
By frosty winter raven nights.

Lullaby

The marigold moon is cradling
on a cherry blossom branch,
Adorning my sleep with floweret fragrances,
And delicate dreams infused with silver stars filigree,
A blushed blue butterfly is covering my silky skin
with a blanket of silence crocheted with lilac lilies.

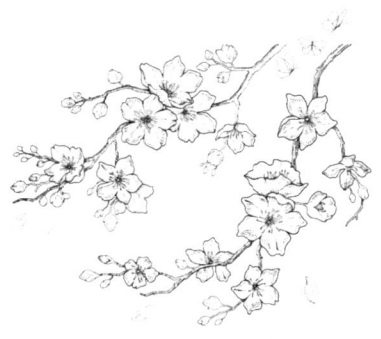

Periwinkle blue

Cruelly crushed under periwinkle blue,
Under its lyrical spells I will subdue,
The nature begs to write about you,
It cries cold tears, but don't have a clue,
How hard is this time to say I love you.

Candyfloss posy

I'll dip my pen in candyfloss posy,
Covering the pages with their subtle scent,
Bluish epiphany, the letters turn to rosy,
Blushing with shyness, in love they melt.

Equinox

Equinox of spring,
The drops of snow,
With snowdrops sing.

Winter gardener

You planted pastel tulips
In the crevasses of my wounded heart,
Like a winter gardener, you're waiting patiently,
For me to bloom in spring.

Spring melodies

When spring will sing its pastel melodies,
And the tears in my eyes will be drying,
Our limerence will bloom with cerise memories,
My winter crushed soul will start its flying.

The time of the butterflies, the new born sun,
Poetical remedy for my lonely heart strings,
I'll flourish like lavender, when we become one,
As you sprinkle your light on my broken wings.

Dark

Resistance

My name is resistance and I sign it with blood,
The power in me flows like a vivid flood,
The road I am walking is the road of fire,
Danger is my perfume, I was born to inspire.

Walk with me

Walk with me on this glorious boulevard,
Like two lost writers drunk with wine,
Our friendship with sparkling ink we'll entwine,
Eternity will find us in a poetical graveyard.

When it rains

When it rains, I hear you whisper,
Come on here and lay unwind,
I will chase away the monster,
Hidden deep inside your mind.

My ghost

You bended my brittle body,
Made it bleed blackened lilacs,
You placed dying roses with fragile thorns,
On my damask scented skin,
You made the stars sing morbid symphonies
And then you named a peony after my ghost.

Jar of hearts

A full jar of hearts,
I collected in time,
Broken and sad,
Happy and divine.

A full jar of hearts
I collected in time,
Too distracted to see,
That they are all mine.

Bleeding sun

This bleeding sun,
Rising upon the graveyard
Of our shattered dreams,
Is pouring melancholy notes
On my broken heart strings.

Mulberry sun

I was laying on the frosted ground
Watching the flowers grow on my chest
The mulberry sun was crying loud,
With a somber eventide I was blessed.

Lost souls

I allure the lost souls,
I desire to fix them,
Save and heal them,
Because I know
How a lost soul feels like.
Where do the lost souls go?
They walk the dark path
Attracted by the color of my pain,
They seem to come to me.

The pain I know

The pain I know,
Makes me take my fractured heart,
And mend is alone,
With seeds of healing,
And stitches of Sakura blossoms,
Still believing and seeking warmth.

The pain I know,
Makes me set fire to my loneliness,
Letting the streaming pains,
That scream in bleeding echoes
Be released as symphonies of joy.

The pain I know,
Makes me walk for miles,
Over minefields,
Risking it all to find myself again.

Crimson destinies

Stab me with your hysterical hyacinths,
Leaving traces of sandalwood on my skin,
A sorrow-scented rose is rising within,
Our crimson inked destinies, distorted labyrinths.

Velveteen Lungs

I am breathing you in,
Serene and quiet,
You are slipping down,
Embalming my trachea,
Like a burial dress of ebony silk.
You reach into my velveteen lungs,
Like a fluid darkened rainbow.
Sprinkling grief
Upon my heart chords,
You are colouring my inner pain,
In raven stains of agony.
I am feeling like
An astronaut in the ocean,
Fighting for his life.

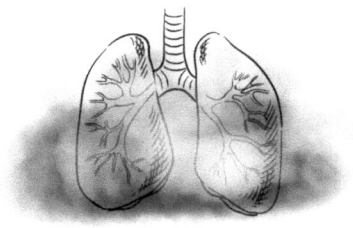

Black queen

Mystique of my mascara and a little black dress,
Like a flower of darkness, in the game of chess,
I'm the bold black queen, noxious beauty of silence,
Tempest of smoky embers, beware of my violence.

Dark euphoria

In the atelier of your never ending doom,
Poisonous chalice of nightmares bloom,
Featherlight lost breaths dissipated in fumes,
Dark euphoria of your intoxicating plumes.

You never knew

You never knew how to save my life,
Just carved my bones with a sharp dark knife,
To make me fit in your perfect fake world,
But then left me breathless without saying a word.

Searching

Time left me wilting under the weeping willow tree,
The wrath of heaven whips with agonising pain,
I wish I found life's worth, but now it's all in vain,
Gasping for air and soulless, I'm still searching for me.

Afterlife

I surrender, I'm hurt, I throw my shield,
I feel my blood drying in this cold wind,
My sword is broken, I've lost this fight,
My wounds are deep, I don't see the light.

I surrender, I'm cold and fervently crying,
No chance to recover and inside I'm dying,
Darkness surrounds me, it's peaceful now,
In front of my fate, I resign with a bow.

I surrender to you my fire full moon,
My eyes are burning, I see my doom,
Protect me forever with your guiding light,
In realms of afterlife I'll continue my fight.

In the darkness

What dwells in the darkness, when you are sleeping,
Silent screaming, screeching, slithering, creeping,
Your dark side is awake, but have no fear,
It's yours to keep, to mend, to hold it near.

The gun

I'm singing a dark slow symphony,
Fogging my brain, feeling melancholy,
Inside the barrel of my fate's gun,
I'm inhaling gun powder for fun.

My guardian

When I'm crying the whole day,
And my world just fades away,
You are there to hold me tight,
And together we can fight.

Bitter tears just fall and fall,
On my trembling shattered soul,
In your warm and sweet embrace,
I will always find my place.

And if our life today will end,
On you, dear dad, I can depend,
In this dark and lonely night,
You will be my guarding light.

Storm chaser

A silent storm chaser came into the night,
His velvet gown of dreams, touching my thigh,
His dusted sapphire haze, igniting stardust,
My inner solar embers, longing for his lust.

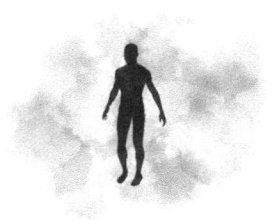

Soldier

Shoot me with the bullets of your poetry,
Stab with me your clever soulless knife,
From this long forgotten cemetery,
I'll come back as a soldier in the afterlife.

Heartbreak casualties, hostages and attacks,
Hidden in my trenches, I'll burn down the tracks,
I'll shelter undercover, but I won't subdue,
Only my aching heart will need a rescue.

Drops of opium

You filled my heart with drops of opium,
Covered in butterscotch sweet toffee words,
Behind your lygophilic noir mask of niobium,
Eldritch horrors and a graveyard of ghosts.

My shadows

Sinister shadows and black specter dreams,
Adrift in the mist, singing silent screams,
My skeletons and secrets will burst the door,
Of this hidden glass casket that I want to ignore.

4 a.m.

My body feels electric, waking in the night,
Empty hazel eyes, glowing in the light,
Vivid astral visions, stirring inner beast,
Brimming with frenzy, I'm hunting for a feast.

The golden key

The golden key to the green gate,
You gave it to me on our first date,
This sacred gift, I had to hide,
Way up the stairs into the night.

The golden key to the green gate,
I lost it last night, oh my cruel fate!
The gothic old tower was dim lit,
The precious key strayed into the pit.

The golden key to the green gate,
I found it again, oh my lucky fate!
It looked so different and it didn't shine,
Behold the change, the green hemlock wine.

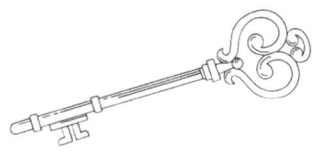

Painted promises

Our cinnamon memories were turned to smoke,
Their hypnotic essence, blew me with a stroke,
Dark vanilla melting, in my broken heart,
Your dulcet painted promises, made me fall apart.

Bold beauty

Graceful and calm, she crosses the street,
I admire her silhouette, just perfect and fit,
She is a bold beauty ... what else can I say?
This little black cat ... just ruined my day.

Gloomy skies

Gloomy skies above, blood moon apparition,
Breaking down my walls, beyond recognition,
Raw emotions evoking, losing my condition,
Labyrinths of heatwave, deadly ammunition.

Sweetpea memories

I will fold myself in raven peony laces,
Whispering my lonely tale in forlorn places,
Wilting slowly in this dusty dark greenhouse,
Your sweetpea memories are now broken vows.

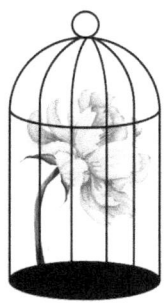

Alpha calls

Throw me to the wolves, as darkness falls,
Noir feelings have possessed your soul,
Creepy creatures, took you under control,
But I'm raising the dead with my alpha calls.

Sad violin song

My sad violin song echoing the woods
Piecing the swan lake, lamenting moods,
The heart is cold, I've been gone astray
Since that gloomy night when you went away.

My sad violin song, is calling you in vain,
My heart is punctured, infused with pain,
Only fluid music flows through my veins,
Going insane, but your memory remains.

Haunted house

This house is haunted by our memories of lust,
My eclipsed heart rests in time's golden dust,
Our paper thin smiles, in sepia colored pictures,
With porcelain hands I'm mending me with
stitches.

My cure

Maybe I'm cursed, but you are my cure,
I'll drink your emerald glowing blood,
My haunted soul will shear its sins,
As my thirst is quenched and the veil thins.

My dreams

My dreams are hiding under the nightmare's cloak,
Sparkling neurones like fireflies are spinning,
Your touch, your kiss, turn my monsters to smoke,
Storm passes when I see your rainbow beaming.

Hourglass

Hidden in this opaline hourglass,
Gathering our sand memories,
The knife of time is stabbing my back,
I just can't stop the time.

Ghosts of my past

Stitching my open skin,
With emeralds and onyx threads,
And embroideries of dusted petals,
Trying to comfort my burning soul,
I hear the ghosts of my past,
Singing lullabies deep out of my core.
They make my darkness shine,
Shimmering like copper and fire,
Then I fade into a nebula haze,
Entwining with their karmic frequencies.

Coffee

Special place

There is a special place inside my heart,
With honeyed hues, inspiring my art,
With walls of caramel and glittery amber,
I welcome you to my „coffee chamber".

Caramel bliss

Reverberant syllables taste like caramel bliss,
Deliciously delirious, my stanzas need a kiss,
Maple droplets on my tongue, the rhyme is sweet,
My ink is liquid honey, my canvas gets a treat.

Cup of poetry

With love pumping through our veins
We cuddle under the warm moonlight,
Over a hot cup of poetry,
We will make peach and passionfruit love,
Until I will be running out of metaphors.

Lavender coffee

I will pour your lavender coffee
Over my rusty heart strings,
I will add a pinch of toffee,
To stick together my broken wings.

Barista love

Hear the melancholic melody of my barista love,
I'll shape the sunlight and cover you, my dove,
Let me take your sadness and make it mine,
In cinnamon gold reflections we will entwine.

Cup of you

My quivering heart needs a cup of you,
I'll let you paint it in burnt butter hue,
You'll warm the dark edges of my soul,
In sunset caramel, you'll cover me whole.

Brewing hearts

Our bodies bathe in waves of latte sheets
Your melodious passion is covering my thighs,
Two brewing hearts, connecting on high beats,
The time stops sudden between our sighs.

Frosted memories

When frosted memories melt away
Their milky taste is here to stay,
The sunset rays caressing us slow,
The tender lights will make us glow.

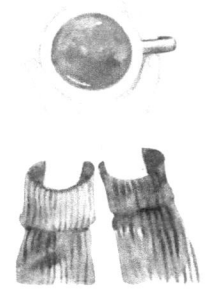

Cinnamon tears

I am here again in your embrace,
I see the love on your sweet face,
I'll taste again your coffee kiss,
Cinnamon tears are just pure bliss.

Sensual sweetness

Wear me like wool, on autumn mornings,
I'll kiss the coffee that caresses your lips,
Sensual sweetness, delicious drippings,
Alluring aromas of tempting fingertips.

Cinnamon skin

I painted October on your cinnamon skin,
Cozy prelude, you caught me in a spin,
Sipping the raindrops from your raspberry lips,
You made me blush, as you touched my hips.

Buttercup skin

Your butterfly caresses trail my buttercup skin,
I crave for your twinkling twilight touch,
Our midnight kisses blossom, you make me spin,
I never thought I would miss your arms so much.

Cozy arms

When the autumn weeps cinnamon tears,
And the singing birds are calling my name,
In your cozy warm arms I'll melt my fears,
We'll burn together into a golden flame.

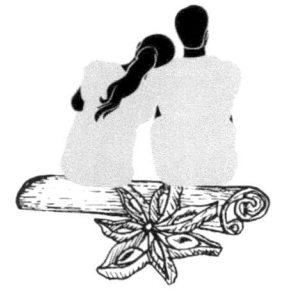

Honeycomb body

Drink my succulent saccharine cinnamon drops,
Forged in the alluring depths of my honeycomb body,
Energise your senses, as we rise to the tops,
Iridescent prelude, our love-making is godly.

Scents of cinnamon

This hole in my heart was filled with scents of cinnamon,
I've been forgetting to breathe, you were my vitamin,
I'm caught up in a bitter sweet September saudade,
The voice of your shadow, plays in the heartbreak arcade.

Essence of summer

I keep the essence of summer like a fanatic,
In a closed night jar, I'm melon-dramatic,
You want to stay, I just want to flee,
Someone, please drown me in more ice tea.

Summer memories

Wearing your shirt, rewinding summer memories,
Bursting bubbles of past and dreamland melodies,
Melting with the lyrics on your lemonade lips,
I'm drinking spells of love in tiny scarlet sips.

Your coffee cup

I am drinking from your coffee cup,
The bitter taste reminds me of you,
How we exchanged some sparks out of the blue,
The wildfire in our hearts was rising up.

Daydreaming

White camellia daydreaming, on a summer day,
Your vintage love embroidery is begging me to stay,
The symphony of our bodies, delicious mocha nights,
Idyllic specks of passion, I'm craving your delights.

Ardent eyes

I see me naked in your ardent eyes,
The way we gleam is no surprise,
Caramel-cup cravings, topped with cream,
Seductive sweet aroma, a delicious dream.

Glitters of September

Smeared with ginger glitters of September,
I am in love with autumn, my sweet surrender,
Allured by the auburn shades of the leaves,
I'll cover me in their cinnamon scented dreams.

My cup of coffee

My cup of coffee sang to me today,
Vanilla in her eyes and a bitter heart,
Her latte tears weeping summer's depart
I held her tight, so she won't go astray.

Autumn heart

Autumn in my heart, with leaf-covered walls,
It's the season of rainboots and umbrellas,
A beautiful haunting through its scarlet halls,
The caramel coziness that slowly installs.

Singing snowflakes

In hiemal days with frosted moon wishes,
With whispers of winter in shades of November,
Singing snowflakes, touching with crisp kisses,
To my chai aromas you'll softly surrender.

Vanilla

The vanilla taste of my skin,
Love embers for your fire within.

Peached mornings

On peached mornings, I'm melting in your glow,
Hot chocolate cups, undress my jumper slow,
You make me feel warm, in winter frosty nights,
Your sugarplum kisses caress my pearly thighs.

Creamy coffee

Sipping slow my creamy coffee,
Let me taste your sticky toffee,
Fill my cup with pure pressed prose,
Swirl your honey on my rose,
Vanilla taste of my blushed red lips,
Ristretto prelude in steamy drips.

Coffee date

When I first met you,
You were hand in hand with poetry,
Words of wisdom were woven,
Around an alluring aura,
Bonding bronzed bodies,
Kindly kaleidoscopic kisses,
Shimmering summer sunsets,
Then you gave your poetry to me,
And we went together for a coffee.

Cosmic

Stardust traces

I have your stardust traces in me,
Because you and I are chemistry,
I stayed so close, tucked in your arms,
We shared some atoms and some charms.

Epiphany of words

Barefoot on the green poetical fields
Of my imagination,
I feel the soft epiphany of words,
Flying wildly like lustrous fireflies,
Hiding wisely in scholastic thoughts,
Trying to find their rest on the velveteen sheets,
Succumbing into fairytale reveries.

Lights

Wearing the kaleidoscope as a map,
I'll travel to undiscovered places,
I'll bring new lights in these lost spaces,
In the crevasses of my broken heart.

Tears of gold

Lipstick stains adorned with tears of gold,
Your stardust soul will wipe them all away,
I'm a „bella donna" when I cry, so I was told,
Wrapped in your caring arms is my getaway.

Pixie dust

Lilac hues of love and lust,
Imprisoned in your silky eyes,
My sweetest soul of pastel dyes,
You're made of dazzling pixie dust.

Fairy of the lunar lake

The fairy of the lunar lake, got lost in a dream,
Of peached sun eclipses and cosmic dust gleam,
Her fears were dancing eerie, like raven butterflies,
The sky, festooned with stars, she was hypnotised.

Her soul was lifting high into the satin night,
Laced in black ribbons, she gave up the fight,
She felt his presence near, holding her tight,
The nightmare was over as she saw his light.

Precious moon

Faithful fragments of my precious moon,
Stirring inside a luscious love monsoon,
Gazing at your hypnotic radiant lights,
I'll be one with you, in my bluish nights.

Song of you

I will always dance to the song of you,
That paints my bare soul in peony hue,
Under this starry neon ambrosial night,
Our shimmering hearts are shining bright.

Pearly feather

I am a pearly feather falling freely to the ground,
Peaceful, fearless, floating without making a sound,
I will soon find my rest for my broken shield,
My ballad of tears, on the dewy gemmed field.

Midnight monsoon

Nectarine sweet lips, I'm your midnight monsoon,
Tangerine tantalising, my skin glows like the moon,
Infused with passion and my pomegranate poetry,
I'm alluring you with my body's symphony.

My tears

My tears are butterflies unfolding rhymes,
The shimmer covered letters, inflaming scrolls,
In lazuline midnights we lost our souls,
I'm drowning in poetry in these fragile times.

Stardust lips

Rose cheeks, white skirt, stardust covered lips,
You search for the heaven covering my hips,
Chasing butterfly dreams, our love is first,
Waltzing tides of romance will quench our thirst.

Viridescent full moon

You guide me through my times of sorrow,
When deadly demons try to catch my mind,
I know that you will still be here tomorrow,
And if I fall again, support in you I'll find.

My viridescent full moon, my guiding light,
The torch of my soul, you shine so bright,
I know I'll always find you, my midnight twin,
Your power, my strength, is rising from within.

Blanketed in stars

Blanketed in stars, I'll watch them shine,
Their delicate reflections will be my shrine,
From stardust I'm born, scintillating glow,
In ashes of evigheden I'll perish slow.

Phoenix fires

Phoenix lambent fires caress my silky skin,
I'm rising above the ashes hidden deep within,
Spreading my wings, release myself from chains,
Fighting for the light, I'm duelling my pains.

If my life was a song

If my life was a song,
It would be chanted by the verbena moon
Waning herself with the reverberation
of the blooming heliotrope stars,
Harmonized by the lonely lullaby
of an auburn nightingale,
And by the diamond dewdrops
falling on a Blue Bayou dahlia petal.

Midnight blues

I am drowning in my midnight blues,
In waves of emotions, dyed in rainbow hues,
I stole the turquoise tears of the butterflies,
Waiting to be saved by the lilac skies.

Silhouettes

We're two silhouettes at sunset, kissing slow,
Counting constellations on each other's skin,
The afterglow serenity fills the place between,
While we surrender, to love's honeyed glow.

Afterglow

Under the iridescent afterglow,
You threw me to the raging waves,
The sky burned wild in silent flames,
Our love turned to ashes, burning slow.

Galaxies of your eyes

I'm lost between the galaxies of your eyes,
I've found my solace in their sparkling maze,
You've painted my heart with their hazel dyes,
And dressed me in stars with your cosmic blaze.

Nostalgic rains

Nostalgic rains are baptizing my bones,
As they slowly fade into raven fumes,
They will ink my poems with stellar plumes
And glow forever for hearts made of stone.

Armour

Nightgown of kisses, petals and butterflies,
Adorns me with ribbons of your soothing skies,
You webbed an armour for my velvet skin,
Coating my dark fears that lurk deep within.

Dreaming daffodils

Sky adorned in twinkling silver stars,
Dreaming daffodils covering my scars,
Nocturnal regrets in a jar of fireflies,
My stelliform soul, a snow angel in your eyes.

Green stars

Heaven is weeping green stars tonight,
We're now traces in the sands of time,
Our ivory towers have lost their sublime,
I'm mourning your music in the moonlight.

Love

Dreamland

I write your name on imagination's tinted glass,
With specks of gold, so we could be forever,
Two petals of hope, a surreal love's surrender,
Trapped in my dreamland, I can't let you pass.

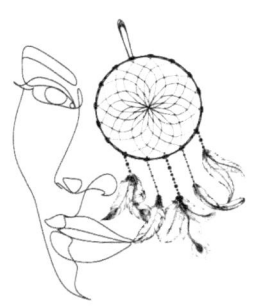

Lavender fields

We were making love in lavender fields,
Counting the clouds as they went by,
Time stood still, around us was blank,
Witnesses were only the clouds in the sky.

My wounds

You have opened my soul,
Glimpsing inside of me
You saw my wounds
Like a valley of peaceful lilies.
Under flickering candles,
You wove an embroidery of petals,
With your strings of love,
Covering them with eternity.

Lambent love

Write poetry on my skin, with luminescent letters,
and radiant rays from your lustrous heart,
Touch my silky skin with your sensual sweetness,
Dripping metaphors under the silver stars,
Look into my eyes and you will find,
My eternal lambent love.

Fifty shades

Fifty shades of emerald tears,
I kissed away from your frosted lips
Pretty, dreamy, dressed in all black,
I'm alluring you with my fingertips.

Neon drops

Your neon drops on my midnight shore,
Paint my skin with resplendent hues,
Our bodies are dancing, synchronised fuse,
Igniting sultry passion is what we adore.

Vintage hearts

We were two velvet vintage hearts,
Laying lonely in sanguine sandcastles,
We found each other in melodious arts,
Entwined in love, we won the fate's battles.

Pastel teasing

Pastel soft teasing, metaphors whipping,
You leave behind amaranthine traces,
Tie me up with your candyfloss laces,
Make love to me, when the moon is sleeping.

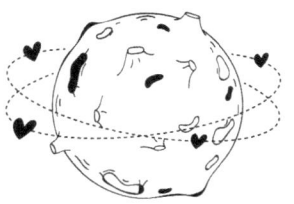

Aurora ardors

Aurora ardors and ocean lullabies,
Your poetry on my skin under sapphire skies,
Our bodies blushing echoes, silent harmonies,
This sentimental summer, magenta memories.

My sunshine

I'm feeling you close, caressing my skin,
Your kisses are gently dancing on my back,
My sunshine is musically flaming within,
This summer you are my favourite soundtrack.

Lustful eyes

I saw his lustful eyes reflected on my skin,
Lilac laced lingerie, my hips, his silent sin,
Sensually soft lips, he will bite them slow,
Blushing tender petals, with his touch, will glow,
Syncing lambent love, through our hearts will flow.

Soft evenings

This sunset reminds me of your blues,
Infused in a profusion of dusky hues,
Our soft evenings on a floral balcony,
On silky sheets, our enchanted symphony.

Summer lover

August was my lover, we were really close,
He left me crying sunshine and bitterly prose,
Under rusty coated skies, autumnal mood,
I feel September coming, his embers burn so good.

Cerulean skies

Beneath cerulean skies with indigo hazes,
My heart is searching for you through ivy mazes,
I won't give up, I'm drawn by your gravity,
Dance me around the moon, change my reality.

Lips dance

Our lips dance again in the rhythm of passion,
Painting on peached sheets, melodical waves,
Skin on skin with you is my new fashion,
One taste of you will satisfy my craves.

Whispering metaphors

Dancing, entwined under the radiant moon,
Your poetry leaves marks on my ruby lips,
Whispering metaphors you're alluring my hips,
We're star-crossed lovers, in a moonlight swoon.

Velcro

As I entered the room,
Passion was levitating,
You grabbed my waistline,
Biting your lips,
And reaching my back
To open the velcro of my dress.

Feeling love

I am feeling love,
Dancing in a new dawn,
Singing quietly to myself that,
I am not afraid of your raging fire,
Crashing me with immortal breaths,
When my heart still lays near yours.

Sonnets of scars

I am in love,
In love with me and my sonnets of scars,
Left behind after feeling so much,
Treasuring even the dark part of me,
Ripping scarlet afterglow sun rays,
To beam warmness on my soul again.

Let me love you

Just let me love you,
From the beginning,
And see what happens
After we collide,
Reveries and butterflies,
Serendipity encounter,
With melancholy fragrance,
A romantic bonding,
A beautiful mess,
In chaotic nights.

Sakura blossom sips

Versatile elixir of Sakura blossom sips,
Dripping on my thirsty vermillion lips,
Plethora of blushed symphonic dreams,
Incandescence of love's radiant gleams.

Raspberry kisses

Raspberry laced kisses, dripping on velvety sheets,
Braided lust, specks of carnations and sweets,
Our entangled bodies, your elixir is quenching,
On tides of blissful passion, our love is dancing.

Flakes of gold

Paint me in flakes of gold
And candy cane kisses,
Like it's the last time we meet,
Cover my damask scented skin
With peony petals,
Make love to me,
Deeply soft and sweet.

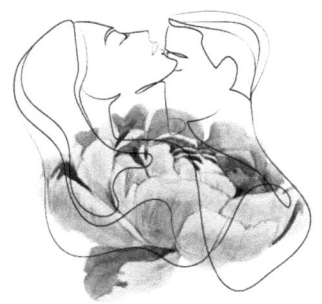

Soft feelings

Mint sparkles on lips, seduce me slow,
Our bluet hearts together will glow,
Bubbling soft feelings they will ignite,
In hues of green, our love we'll recite.

Elegant failure

Lavender snow flakes falling on the ground,
Black onyx mascara trickling down my face,
I'm an elegant failure without your embrace,
Lost in this daydream, I crave to be found.

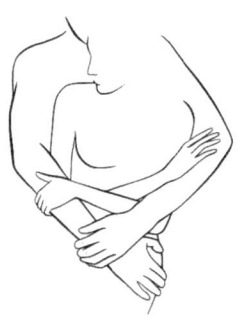

Fix me

You've opened a wound in me,
So deep that I could see
The iridescent sparkles
Coming from my heart's abyss.
Trying to mend what's left of me,
You're rearranging the fractures,
Closing them, fixing them,
Repainting the stained broken glass
Without knowing that
Through those cracks,
The light comes inside of me,
Shimmering dreamy rainbows
In my palace of lavender and lace.

Tattoo

My viridescent reflection on your velvet heart,
Will blossom eternal, through your spellbinding art,
I'll let you paint me in spring hues of you,
Keeping you forever like a glowing tattoo.

I found July

I found July in your deep brown eyes,
Got trapped with you in dreamland…no…in paradise!
You caressed my skin with daisies and spells of delight,
Then we melted together into the summer night.

Laconic

Laconic,
The sparkle in your eyes,
Capturing the afterglow rays,
Under the amorous sky.
I hide myself in your shadow,
Embracing you,
To hear your heart beating for me.
I just stay there in the safety,
Of your arms,
Our hearts entwined for eternity.
We let our eyes talk,
Scintillating desire,
While we are still falling in love.

Painted August

I painted August on your sun tanned skin,
Sipping the sea waves from your juicy lips,
You made me spin as you touched my hips,
I'm both your angel and your deepest sin.

Dreams

I am writing poems on the grass dew,
Walking barefoot on the map of your heart,
I'm caught in a moment of time with you,
Within the walls of this dream and never apart.

Love blooms

Our love blooms in the poems I write,
On the blank pages our hearts will ignite,
My verses are sparkling in crimson and pink,
Our bodies entwined with grace will sync.

Heart chords

My heart chords are made of whispers,
Of pastel scars and peaceful glisters,
Amber skies of healing are soothing my soul,
They caress my nights, they bring me hope.

You are my hope

My fears consume me but you are my hope,
My demons awaken, you're my reason to cope,
I'm nothing but chaos, you help me survive,
Through days of darkness together we strive.

Little flower

Looking at me from the outside,
I see myself like a little flower,
Preparing to find the solace of spring.

Fragile creature,
Darling bud of love,
Surrounded by your sunshine,
And your dusky luminous eyes.

Blossoming in hues of rose and green,
Stained with rainbow,
With scarlet clouds dancing above,
Your soft touch caresses me,
Promising me a touch of eternity,
Our melting hearts will florescence with hope.

Orange dipped words

Orange dipped words, an autumn rhapsody,
Flowing on auburn leaves, November's harmony,
They will soon find peace, my soul needs remedy,
Stanzas with crisp rhymes, imprinted ardently.

Hibernated hearts

Hibernated hearts, healing hues,
Sun kissed snowflakes, rhythmic blues,
Frosted tears with diamond sparks,
Alluring winter, our love leaves marks.

Melt my frozen heart

Melt my frozen heart, with your gentle touch,
My amber autumn lover I crave your warmth so much,
Covered in your arms, the whispers of fire glow,
Sensually softly entwined, waiting for the snow.

Your prose is on my lips, iridescent desires,
Burn again my thoughts with your inner fires,
Under the laced mistletoe, I vow my love forever,
I'll stay inside with you in this cold December.

Overdose of you

Overdose of you, running through my veins,
Echoing my name, putting me in chains,
Reaching to my brain, release me of my pains,
Whirling lustful love, feeling how it reigns.

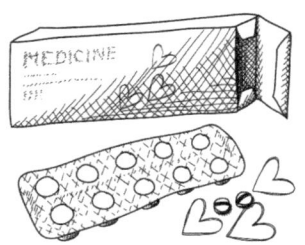

Paint my dreams

Pastel promises whispered with your lips,
Paint my dreams with stardust of your fingertips,
I see hues of harmony locked up in your eyes,
Hold my heart forever under amber skies.

Wait for you

Touching this void in my heart,
I would fill it with scarlet skies,
Pastel pearlescent feathery clouds,
Agate and aquamarine eclipses,
Whispering marigolds, lilacs and daffodils,
Four-leaf clovers, blooming bourbon butterflies,
And frozen fractals of opaline snow flakes,
With secrets left unsaid, regurgitating regrets,
And bubble promises.
When I am done,
I will hide under the lavender moon,
Adrift in the snow obsidian mist,
Between the wild roses, like a wandering ghost,
And wait for you to return.

Before you came

Before you came there was a torn star in me,
I was bleeding bourgeois petals, I was a lost lonely moth,
My obsidian heart was weeping forlorn tears dreadfully,
As you fluttered into my arms and kissed you,
I knew I found in you my gleaming light,
My piece of heaven.

Diamond scars

I feel you like diamonds engraved on my skin,
Unraveling the secrets hidden within.
Blithe crevasses of lushness stories,
Of fears and tears, of golden glories.

I used to paint you in hues of me,
To hide you away, so no one could see,
But then I let you burst out loud,
You make me stronger, I let you shout.

I'm proud of you, I will let you be,
As you just make me, a better me.

Stars in you

Let me enlighten stars in you,
Their periwinkle haze will caress your nights,
They'll hold your fragility and your lonely sighs,
The scars that you bear, I'll make them bloom.

Forever with you

Forever with you through grace and fire,
I see my reflection in your dark brown eyes,
Longing for your midnight scent is my desire,
Let's paint our days with pastel velvet skies.

Fireflies

I knew that love means feeling the butterflies,
But his love made me feel the fireflies.

Love me in lavender

Love me in lavender
Fields of amber and amethyst,
Souls igniting in passion berry flames,
Touching lips of purple orchids.
Hand in hand in dreamer's hideaway,
Whispering mellifluous love poems,
Ardent caresses on sheets of Egyptian cotton,
Our hearts, in tandem, crimson twin flames.

Last poem

If this was my last poem, I'll be dying,
Waves of melancholy, endless crying,
My tears will be rivers, endless flowing,
Into an ebony testimony, I'll be folding.

The book is not quite finished,
keep reading as on the next pages
I have some surprises for you!

The next four poems belong to my father who was also very passionate about writing when he was 18 trying to impress his Romanian language teacher by scribbling poetry.

A few years later, one special lady was definitely impressed by his poems, my mom.

I have translated them from Romanian and through my book
I am fulfilling one of his great wishes, to publish a book.

I love you Dad!

In his loving memory

Tears in the sun

Between tears, black butterflies
And us,
Is you,
Between tears, black butterflies
And us,
A blue sun was implored for eternity,
Between tears, black butterflies
And us,
I am looking at truth's innocence,
Between tears, black butterflies
And us,
It will always be you!

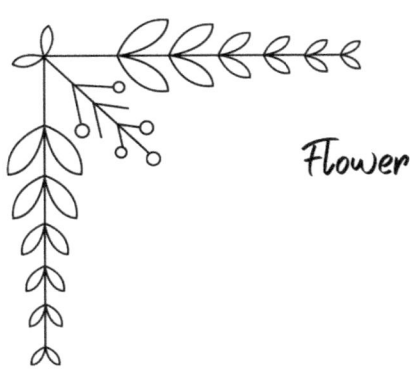

Flower

Everyone is born
By picking up a flower,
Every flower is born,
Gaining her innocence,
Everyone is alone
Until a flower calls him,
And the flower will give up her life
To define herself beside him as a human.

Illusion

You offered me a teardrop ,
Fallen on an apple branch,
To gaze through it,
The sorrow of the sun,
But I know...
I will behold only then,
When the leaves of the tree,
Will be rife with tears of dew.

Am I living ?

Today I tried to fly for the first time.
It wasn't easy,
First I have jumped up,
then
I have jumped over the fence,
And finally I have jumped
Over death.

Special appreciation and gratitude for a
very talented soul
who supported me always with her heartwarming
words and sincere friendship,
Amanda Hearn.

The next page is dedicated to her in form of
a book feature.

Please follow her Instagram page
@amanda_hearn49
to meet her magical heartfelt poetry.

Peace meets me at sunrise

Peace meets me at sunrise,
As coffee coated, burnt bronze rays,
Slumber in coruscate haze,
And reams of liquid light beams,
Blaze, under caramelised skies,
Promises paint my dreams,
With mocha woods and cocoa clouds,
Where velvet violets
Bathe in copper streams,
Beneath the gaze, of sunlight's crown
And radiant halcyon halos,
Rise to meet the dawn,
As moonshine's mellow memory,
Fades to greet the mounting morn.

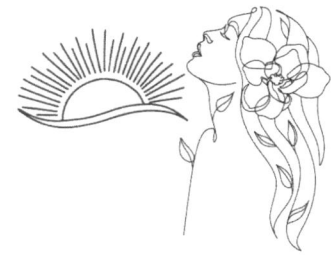

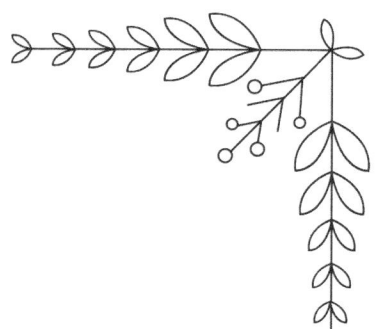

On the next two pages I have added two „@fairy.world.poetry"
collaborations that I deeply care about.
I hope you will enjoy them and I hope that they will make
you to still believe in fairytales.

One of them is with @zahra_abraham, inspired by
„The Beauty and the Beast" and the other one is with
@frogpezografia inspired by „Cinderella".

Please check out the Instagram pages of these two amazing
and talented poets that are also my friends.

Special „Thank you" for them for always being
an inspiration for me.

Evergreen embers engraved upon her heart,
Her dazzling decadent dreams torn apart,
Pearlescent prince of chaos and calm,
Her golden shimmering soul he did embalm,
Turbulent trinkets her heart treasures,
Mystical muse of her poetical pleasures,
Bleeding bronze dew drops of sorrow,
Lost is her amber autumn glow of tomorrow.
@zahra_abraham

She saw autumn ambers in his dazzling eyes,
Falling for him, floating in love, she is mesmerized,
His heart full of treasures, she will discover,
Pearlescent prince, her strength will uncover,
His bronze dew drops of pains, she had caressed,
Turbulent mystical past, he had confessed,
His shimmering soul, shelved from the fall,
Their twin flame limerence had conquered it all.
@fairy.world.poetry

When you're broken and bleeding blue,
Hurting, hopeless in helpless hue,
Lean on me I will help you through,
I will hold and heal and hug you too.
All of this you already knew
My princess my love is true,
Remember it is I who found your shoe
And that is what lead me to you.
@frogpezografia

You found my shoe and won my heart,
I sensed your love right from the start,
There's no more bleeding blue for me,
My charming prince, you're all I see.
You came to cast away this spell,
In your healing embrace I hide so well,
My hurting heart has lost it's veil,
Our happy ending, in this fairytale.
@fairy.world.poetry

My next surprise for you is a truly heartwarming poem dedication from a kind soul, Hiya Sharma. She wrote this poem for me when my heart was darkened by grief and embalmed it with her words. You can find Hiya's ,,whimsical wonderland" poems on Instagram, on her 2 pages:

@soulful_poetry_from_the_heart

@_the.vintage.wand_

Coral blue fireflies shimmer in golden lost lyrics,
Cradling her spirit in aliferous silver of
Aurora Borealis,
Cocooned in almond hours of reminiscences,
a rufescent vetiver wish glows,
Crestfallen syllables echo in synonymous sonority,
where her romanian mauve moon
still whispers a love that bestows.
Lambent like lustrous lavender gloss,
she paints her fairytale buds amidst ordeal olives,
Juniper fragrances of walnut forest,
may have laced her hibiscus heart,
But, purple phosphorescence and violet vintage
dreams are her soulful vicinals,
For albeit this synthetic sombre spring,
she's an emerald ephemeral.
Although coral blue fireflies simmer
in solemn lost lyrics
She's a brilliant blushed butterfly,
who is rekindled and blissfully born.

Credit for the prompts I have used in some of my poems,
goes to the following amazing Instagram Pages:

@altpoetryprompts
@abiertoreino
@bleedingink_mistress
@coralynn.poetry
@donna.jill26
@frogpe3ografia
@fallspoetry
@fragementspoetry
@libby.jenner.poetry
@lonelylines.poetry
@ohmypoems
@oliviabellapoetry
@poeticreveries
@portofpoetry
@poets_island
@poeticgardener1
@soulful_poetry_from_the_heart
@_seya._
@the.ethers.tragic
@zahra_abraham_

I am grateful for the inspiring prompts and support you
have offered me!

Thank you for taking your precious time
to read my poems.
But don't close the book just yet, because
on the next pages there is a
special notes and draw area.

It's your turn to get creative and have fun by writing
your own poems/ideas. As you will notice there is a
notes/draw/color page for each chapter.

If I inspired your muse feel free to send me your
poems on one of my Instagram pages:
@_the.ephemeral.soul_
@fairy.world.poetry
and I will share your creation for you.
If you enjoyed my bookI kindly invite you to leave a
review on Amazon and Goodreads, it will help my book
thrive and find other readers.
Thank you in advance for your support!

Notes

Notes

Notes

Notes

Notes

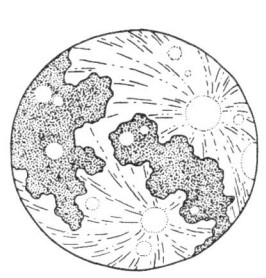

Notes

One more surprise for you: 2 bookmarks
to cut, draw and enjoy!
You can also glue them on cardboard paper so that
they can have a longer life!

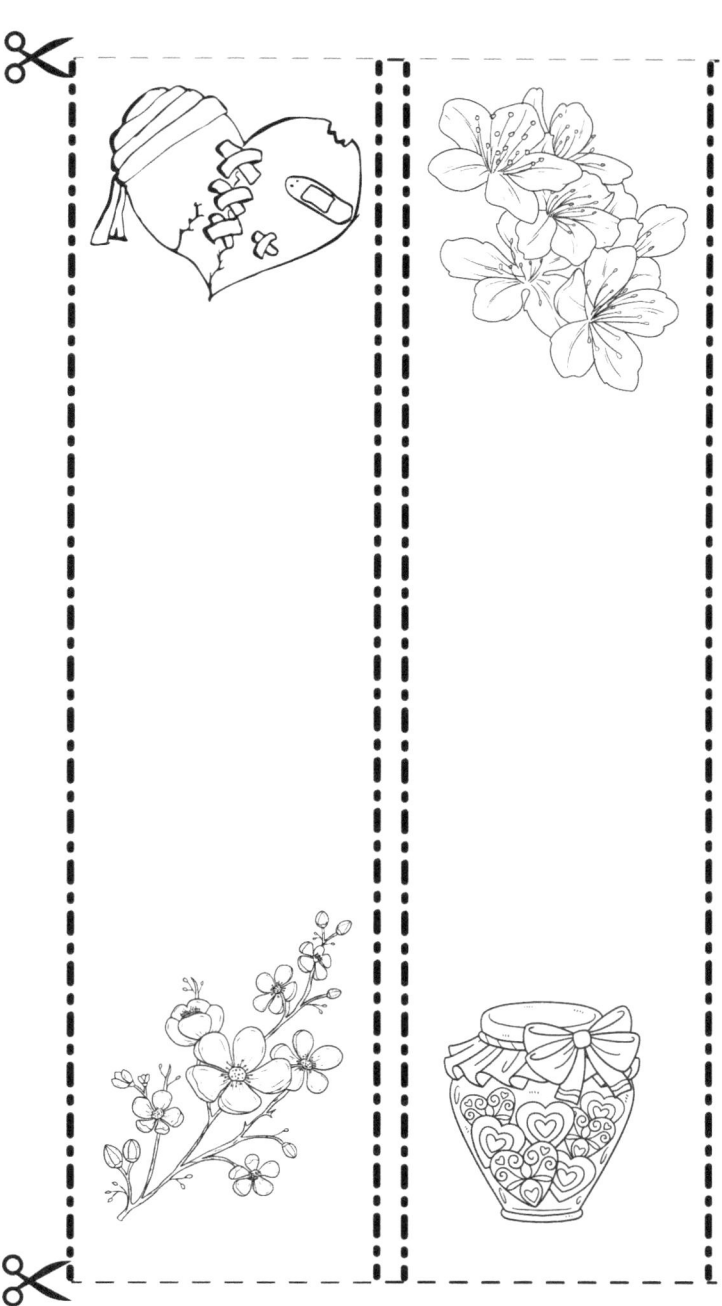

Chapters

"Poetry"
"Flowers"
"Dark"
"Coffee"
"Cosmic"
"Love"

Each 2 chapters form 3 phrases: "Poetry flowers" "Dark Coffee" and "Cosmic Love" but there can also be other combinations ,,Dark flowers", ,,Love coffee", ,,Cosmic poetry"

...can you find some more?

In the same „Tiny Thoughts" Collection
I have also published two journals.
One is dedicated to all the creative souls that
have been through a Writer's block and the
other one is a „Motivational Notebook"
because we all need some kind advice every
now and then.
They are both 4x6 inches and they perfectly
pass in your purse/bag.
Hope that they will bring you solace and
inspiration!

Sending my love to you,
Alexandra

Don't
give up on
yourself

Sending my love,
Alexandra